Compassionate Purpose

DISCOVERING A LIFE OF
FULFILMENT

Andrea Putting

Melbourne - Australia

In our unsettled and anxious world, Andrea Putting's new book provides a clear path that will assist you in identifying your compassionate purpose. This book is well written and provides inspiring stories, useful resources and tools to help you find your strengths, stories and, more importantly, your social legacy. Listen to Andrea's 'voice' guide you in asking the searching questions to find your chosen path so that you can become an authentic influencer. As Andrea notes, the world is crying out for love and compassion, and in these pages, she challenges us all to respond by finding and living our own compassionate purpose. If the world is to change, we all need to do this work.

Dr Lynne Reeder, National Lead, Australian Compassion Council

The recipe for a productive life is to have a purpose. **This book unlocks the secrets by providing tools to find your unique way of impacting others** that brings gratification and contentedness.

Troy Gray – Founder Charity TV Global

Compassionate Purpose is a must read for those looking to fulfil their ultimate purpose. With poetic prose and joyful stories, Andrea guides us through practical steps that stir the flames and stokes the fire within long after the reader has put the book down. It is on that I will revisit again and again.

Heather Joy Basset – Business and Life Strategist

First published in 2022 by **Putting Words.**

© Andrea Putting, 2022

The moral rights of the author have been asserted.

All rights reserved except as permitted under the Australian Copyright Act 1968 (for example, fair dealing for the purposes of study, research, criticism or review). No part of this publication may be reproduced, distributed, or transmitted in any form or by any means, including photocopying, recording, or other electronic or mechanical methods, without the author's prior written permission. All requests should be made through the publisher at the address below.

Putting Words
PO Box 5062
Wonga Park, Victoria, Australia. 3115
www.puttingwords.com
books@puttingwords.com

A catalogue record for this book is available from the National Library of Australia.

ISBN: 978-0-6454591-6-6 (Paperback)
ISBN: 978-0-6454591-7-3 (E-book)
ISBN: 978-0-6454591-8-0 (Hardback)

Produced by **Putting Words**
Cover design by Ashish Joshi
Edited by Anna Von Zinner

Other books by Andrea Putting

Awakened Stealth Leadership
A Soulful Approach to
Growing People and Organisations

Compassionate Prosperity
When Success Is Not Enough

Moment of Infinity
An Anthology of Daily Devotions

Contents

Preface..5

Acknowledgements...9

Compassionate Purpose...................................13

Creating a Legacy 21

It's All About You 27

Beyond the Why 37

Stories from the Podcast...................................45

The Languages of Social Mission 67

Uncovering Your Ultimate Impact 77

You Are Not Enough..101

Follow Your Heart 107

Bibliography..113

Index..115

About the Author 117

Chocolate and Coffee Breaks 121

Social Mission Revolution Podcast 123

*Dedicated to my Mum and Dad,
Lyanne and Harry Putting
who are my greatest
social mission mentors
and role-models.*

Preface

The pieces lie on the table. What is the picture they make? Random shapes of the puzzle wait to be put together.

The stories of our lives are like a puzzle. They often feel like they are random and have no connection. One by one, we pull all the pieces into place. Sometimes they are hard to connect. There is always that piece that seems not to fit anywhere. Look at the image and colour. Where does it go? How does it belong in the picture?

Maybe it doesn't belong. Perhaps it is just a random extra piece.

Specific colours catch your attention. The images are clear, and you quickly pull these together. These are the favourite parts of your journey. Can't all the pieces be like this, bright and filled with joy? But the puzzle is incomplete. Other colours aren't so appealing. The images may be in the shadows. These, too, need to be added to give you the whole picture.

More and more of the picture is revealed as the puzzle comes together. Those pieces you didn't like so much suddenly come alive. They fill in the blanks helping it all make sense. On their own, they weren't so appealing; suddenly, together, you see the beauty in them. They have made you who you are today.

Each part of your life is a part of a puzzle that, when pieced together, helps you to discover who you are.

Finding a purpose in life is like doing a puzzle. Piece by piece, it comes together. We can't just look at our favourite memories. Every part of life needs to come together to find the common threads. When all the pieces are in place, then we can find our purpose.

Compassionate Purpose is the journey into finding the purpose that takes hold of you. It picks you up and takes you in a direction that may have never occurred to you. It shouts out to you with compulsion. No matter how hard you try to turn it off, it is always there, tugging at you. Here is the something that you *can't not do*. You MUST do it.

With all your might, you will follow this. Once you step into its stream, it will bring you a new way of being. Here you will find your most extraordinary sense of worth and purpose. Your life is fulfilled as you discover the *art of giving of yourself*.

When I developed my social mission, Chocolate and Coffee Day for Religious Harmony, something happened within me. By finding a purpose that had no apparent benefits to me personally, I discovered a drive within me that became a force of its own. Here was something I can't not do. It picked me up when I was down and got me out of bed. It gave me a reason to do things out of my comfort zone.

The fascination of "**I can't not do this**" led me on this journey. I wanted to explore what it is about a social mission that excites people in their daily life and business. As a result, the Social Mission Revolution was born.

This book is an invitation to consider the legacy you want to live today and leave for generations to come. What is right for you at this time? Where is the future calling you to go? How can you become an **Authentic Influence** whose legacy ripples throughout time and beyond?

Acknowledgements

I acknowledge and pay respect to the Wurundjeri Woi-wurrung people of the Kulin Nation, the Traditional Owners of the land where I live, work and find my inspiration. I pay my respects to Elders past, present and emerging of the Aboriginal and Torrens Strait Islanders. I acknowledge their deep connection to this land, water and the spirit of this place. I celebrate the stories, culture, and traditions of those who have led the way and taught us the importance of community and collaboration to build a better world.

I acknowledge the Social Mission Revolutionists who have heard the call and have responded. They are the ones who are making the difference in a world that needs to be made. They have seen a need and are working to fulfil it.

This journey isn't always easy. It can be a rocky road with long and tiring hours. There can be heartbreak along the way. However, their heart is filled with knowing that they are doing something worthwhile and living a **Compassionate Purpose**.

A special thanks to the guests on my podcast, *Social Mission Revolution*, who constantly inspire and motivate me to keep going. This book would not have been possible without them.

Thank you to my friends and family who have walked this path with me and listened to my craziness.

You give but little when you give
of your possessions.
It is when you give of yourself
that you truly give.

—Kahlil Gibran, The Prophet

Follow Your Heart.

CHAPTER 1

Compassionate Purpose

Follow your heart. The message came over and over again. I had come to that fork in the road when everything was up for questioning.

"What is my purpose? Why am I here? "

The feelings of success and fulfilment in life had been fleeting. They had sent me bouncing around from one thing to another. It was time to find what I was supposed to do with this life. How could I find meaning and purpose?

These are not my questions alone. I hear them time and time again. We all want to make a difference and have a meaningful life. However, finding the answers isn't easy.

It was 2014 when I started my search. I was unemployed and looking for that something to inspire me and give me direction. Suddenly I was offered free psychic readings—

seven of them. OK, I'll take a free reading. Hopefully, they will guide me on what to do next.

The message I received was the same each time. "Follow your heart."

Great. What's that? How do I follow my heart? Can you give me a little more insight? I had no idea. I had to sit with it for some time. I needed to allow myself to discover what my heart was calling me to do.

I listened and responded to what was being presented to me step by step. It led me to discover nothing is more fulfilling than a **Compassionate Purpose**. When we give ourselves to others, our life has meaning and brings us the greatest sense of fulfilment and joy.

The *Social Mission Revolution* podcast has been a part of the journey. As my interest and fascination grew with discovering my **Compassionate Purpose**, I wanted to explore the what, the why and the how.

Those who I talk with who are actively involved in social missions are the people who live rich and fulfilling lives. Their passion is evident and flows freely through them.

When you find your social mission, no matter how big or small, you find the answer to the questions we all ask, "What is my purpose? Why am I here?"

WHAT IS THE SOCIAL MISSION REVOLUTION?

A Social Mission is an overarching phrase that refers to taking up a cause that is not for profit. It is about doing something for others. I refer to it as being in service to other people and the community. Others use "giving back" or "paying it forward." Whatever you call it, it is about making a difference in the world. It is often described as a higher calling. This is your **Compassionate Purpose.**

A social mission can take on many faces, as represented by the various examples on my *Social Mission Revolution* podcast. It can vary from:
- contributing time to charitable events;
- donating funds or gifts;
- volunteering;
- reaching out to someone in need;
- starting a cause or movement.

There are as many ways to have, express and explore social missions as there are people. It can be a grand undertaking or simply offering what you can, your skills, talents or time.

Social missions are embraced by individuals, groups, communities, organisations, businesses and corporations. It spans all sectors, walks of life, cultures, and countries.

As someone with a social mission, you will inspire others, whether you intend to or not. People will notice something special about you. They will connect with someone worth knowing, maybe not even knowing why. What you are doing is serving humanity. You are an **Authentic Influence**.

To be involved in the *Social Mission Revolution*, all that is required is a desire to make a difference and do something greater than yourself.

"Revolution" means "a radical and pervasive change in society and social structure." People who embrace the *Social Mission Revolution* have an overriding sense of wanting to do something more than they have been doing.

Our society has transformed into a materialistic world, where everything is "me" based and "what can I achieve to get more for me." More and more people are turning within and realising that if that world is to be a better place, it is up to us. As Mahatma Gandhi said, "Be the change you want to see in the world."

Revolution also refers to "a turning around as if returning back to a starting point." We are returning to who we truly are by focusing on a social mission. In South Africa, they use the word – *Ubuntu*, which means "I am because you are." It focuses on working together to create a community that is one and a world we all want. For humanity to survive, we must care for each other.

WHY?

Mason looks at me with those big blue eyes. Ever curious, his three-year-old brain is far beyond its years. "Why," he asked me. How many times in one day do I have to answer the "why" question? This time, it was "Why is it raining?" Did he want or need the full explanation of the rain cycle? Or to know the importance of rain to each of us and the planet? Or do I simply say to make puddles? Everything is about puddles.

Once a week, I get to spend the day with my two grandchildren, Mason and his little sister Zoey, aged one. It is a day of wonder, play and often even a little Grandma frustration as I attempt to keep them busy without too much mud.

The question "why" is common amongst toddlers. They want to understand the world. It is not enough to tell them something or ask them to do a task; they want to know all the ins and outs. What is the purpose of doing this? What do I get out of it? Or why shouldn't we do it?

This is how they learn to be decision-makers. This is how they learn about life. So, why after why is asked.

I try to answer as best I can. Sometimes it's not easy because the only way I can think to answer won't satisfy his curiosity. To say something like, "Because I said so," would only teach him to stop asking.

He can only move to the next thing when his curiosity has been satisfied.

I talk about going **Beyond the Why**, letting go of the why and listening to where the future is guiding you. However, continually answering the why questions for Mason has reminded me that we need to understand what is going on to make the most of moving forward.

Compassionate Purpose is one of those things that many people don't understand. Some don't need to. They're just into it. They will serve wherever they can. Their hand is raised for every opportunity that opens up for them.

When the world constantly asks so much of us, it can be difficult to contemplate a **Compassionate Purpose**. You are a busy person. You have commitments to meet and family to support. Finding time for anything else is often out of the question.

This is why you need to understand the why of **Compassionate Purpose** and how it can change your world. It can give your life a sense of meaning. It can lift you and can bring you back into being yourself.

Compassionate Purpose doesn't have to be something that takes time or effort. What it does need to be is something that speaks to your heart and values. When you find the right one for you, it energises and inspires you. You will find in this something you just *can't not* do. It will call out to you wherever you are. It has captured you, and you just have to do it.

When this happens, you will find the greatest fulfilment in life.

In this book, I will share with you the why and how to find your **Compassionate Purpose.** Take your time to explore your thoughts and ideas. Then let them go and allow the future to guide you to finding the **Compassionate Purpose** intended for you.

Meanwhile, I will continue to answer Mason's why questions knowing that one day all his whys will take him "**Beyond the Why**."

Make your story one that will be retold for generations.

Chapter 2

Creating a Legacy

Frank McKinney is a seven-time Bestselling Author in six different genres. He's a Real Estate Artist, Philanthro-Capitalist and Aspirational Speaker. I spoke with him on my podcast, *Social Mission Revolution*, and he shared his story with me.

Frank is very successful at what he does, designing and building beautiful properties that sell for millions of dollars. He has everything he could want and has achieved all of his goals.

After he had sold the most expensive spec home in Palm Beach, his life felt empty. From a business standpoint, he was on top of the world. However, he had lost the heart and soul of it. He had reached a low point and felt like giving it all away.

"Why do I feel like shit?" he asked his coach. His coach was wise and told him, "You need to find your spiritual highest calling, Frank. You've got the professional down pat."

Armed with this challenge, Frank pulled together all of his skills, strengths and business acumen and found them redirected to another purpose. He now builds whole villages in Haiti in areas of need.

The villages contain everything they need – homes, schools, hospitals, community centres, etc. Frank doesn't go in and take over.

He communicates with the people of the village and provides them with the support they need to build their community. He feels it is essential for them to use their skills and knowledge to give them a sense of pride and ownership.

Frank found a new purpose in life. His business now provides the means to do the work he loves.

To hear Frank's journey, listen to the podcast
www.SocialMissionRevolution.com/Frank-McKinney

It could be easy to shrug off this story and say, "Frank is a rich man and can do whatever he wants. I don't have the time or money to follow my passions." However, I have spoken to others with similar stories on the podcast.

They have lost their passions in life and feel like nothing is worthwhile anymore. When they turn it around and engage in a social mission, their lives become inspirational, and they are an **Authentic Influence**.

AUTHENTIC INFLUENCE

In the 21st century, it is easy to become an influencer. You go online, spout a lot of stuff, grow a following, and suddenly become an influencer. It doesn't matter what you say or even if it makes sense. People are following. Is that the kind of influence you want to have in the world? Or do you want to have **Authentic Influence**?

Do you want the influence that comes from doing something good in the world, being true to your values and creating a loyal tribe? When you have **Authentic Influence**, you can unleash your ultimate impact on the planet. Then you have a legacy worth living (and leaving).

Take a minute. Think about the people in your life who have influenced you. Those who have made a profound impact in your life may have changed the way you think, act or the outcomes you have achieved.

In most cases, it won't be some celebrity pushing their agenda. It will be a teacher, mentor or someone who has done something to touch your heart or spoke to your values in life. It is that person who gave you some extra time, had some words that hit the spot, or simply lived their values daily.

I have the privilege of speaking with amazing people on my podcast, *Social Mission Revolution*. These people genuinely are authentic influencers. They live each day to its fullest. They have heard a calling beyond themselves. As they see a need to be filled, they step up to the challenge and take it on. They are making a difference in the world.

When I hear their stories, I am constantly inspired to do something more myself. Each one of them influences me and the way I live my life. They, indeed, are the authentic influencers of the world.

As an **authentic influence**, your legacy will be set. Each day you live a life worth living and leaving. Make your story one that will be retold for generations.

WHAT LEGACIES DO YOU LIVE WITH?

A lot of people talk about leaving a legacy. They want to do something that their children, grandchildren and future generations will be proud of.

What am I proud of when I think about my family and those who have gone before me?

I am proud of my Great Uncle, Albert Siebel, who started the PURA milk company in 1947. He saw a need and fulfilled it. The dairy farmers, at the time, had to transport their milk to the city by horse and cart every day and sell it individually.

He created the company to make their lives easier by collecting milk from the farms and selling it in the city. The company today is very removed from where it was when he retired and sold it. Even though there is no longer any family interest in the company, I am proud of this legacy.

I am proud of my Estonian grandfather, who came to Australia in 1927. He endured a lot in his home country that he never spoke of. When World War II broke out, even though he was officially past the age for enlistment and not an Australian citizen, he wrote countless letters to the Defence Department, volunteering to do his bit for his adopted country. Eventually, they accepted him as he was a skilled tradesman. He was also a great supporter of new immigrants as they sought refuge after the war.

I am proud of my parents for the work they have done, touching the lives of others. People often tell me stories of my father and what a "great man" he was. Through his work within his church ministry, working with homeless people and supporting my mother's work, he left a legacy of great compassion.

My mother continues to touch many lives in many ways, especially when she was the Victorian Director of Camp Quality. This charity provides a camping program for children with cancer.

Legacy is not necessarily about leaving great wads of money. I certainly haven't received any. It is about living a life of **Authentic Influence**, doing things that speak to your heart and that your family can be proud of for generations to come.

Some businesses are maintained in families for generations. A hotel in Japan has been in the one family since 710. (No, I didn't leave a "1" out!) Talk about a legacy!

To leave a legacy like this, a business has to live its values daily. It has to be enjoyable, and the family needs to feel that these values are worthwhile and matter.

I want to leave a legacy for my grandchildren. I want them to be proud of my work and the books I have written. I want them to be proud of the lives I touch and the stories I tell.

I proudly shared with my children as we were shopping how their great-great uncle had started the PURA milk company, and we enjoyed the exploration of the Defence Force archives to uncover the stories of their great-great-grandfather.

I want my grandchildren to proudly share with the world that their grandmother started *Chocolate and Coffee Breaks* and the *Social Mission Revolution*. Every life I touch is part of their story. Every story is their legacy. For them, I need to be an **Authentic Influence** in the world.

What is the legacy you want to live and leave?

CHAPTER 3

It's All About You

How can it be all about me? I'm too busy giving to everyone else; I forget my needs. My focus is on how I can serve. What can I do for others?

True, some of us are over-givers. However, there is a reason why some of us take our **Compassionate Purpose** to the extreme.

Altruism is an interested and selfless concern for the well-being of others, even at the cost of oneself. Many say that true altruism can never exist, as there is always a payback for us.

Let's get real; it feels good. When we help others and give ourselves, we are rewarded by how we feel. In fact, it can be as pleasurable as having sex!

A team of neuroscientists led by Dr Jorge Moll of the National Institutes of Health in the USA found that, what is as pleasurable as having sex, is being altruistic. When research subjects were encouraged to think of giving money to a charity, parts of the brain lit up that are usually associated with selfish pleasures like sex.

We are hard-wired to be altruistic. Put another way, it's difficult for humans to be genuinely selfless because generosity feels so good. So, let's accept and embrace it. It is all about you.

We all want to make a difference. It is inbuilt within us. It is what makes society and community work. We need to feel that our lives have been worthwhile and that something we have done is meaningful to someone else. It is what gives us a sense of purpose and fulfilment in life.

I have found that if we aren't living our purpose in a way that benefits others and is meaningful to someone else, we are always searching for something else. Something that will give us purpose, fulfilment and the feeling that we have done something worthwhile in life.

I was chatting with a friend on the phone one day, and he said, "For the first time, I feel like I'm making a contribution." This friend had just turned 71, and only now that he had been able to turn his focus in life to working with a charity was he finding that deep sense of fulfilment that we all long for.

He had spent his whole life working hard, mostly in his businesses, participating fully in the community, giving and sharing wherever possible. However, never reaching that deep place within him allowed him to feel that he was doing something worthwhile that made that difference that we all long to make.

Dr Stephen Post, founder of the Institute of Research into Unlimited Love and author of *Why Good Things Happen to Good People*, has studied the benefits and links between altruism, compassion, happiness, healing and health for nearly two decades. In *It's good to be good: 2011 5th annual scientific report on health, happiness and helping others,* he points out that happiness, health and even longevity are benefits that have been reported in more than 50 investigations using a variety of methodologies.

In a survey Dr Post conducted of 4,582 American adults, 41 per cent volunteered an average of two hours per week; 68 per cent of volunteers agree that volunteering "has made me feel physically healthier", and 96 per cent say volunteering "makes people happier." In addition, the survey results indicated that volunteers have less trouble sleeping, less anxiety, and better friendships and social networks.

Based on scientific research, Dr Post concludes that giving and even just thinking about giving in a spirit of generosity are linked to health and well-being, and altruism is associated with a substantial reduction in mortality rates and is linked to longevity.

So, if we want to live a happy, healthy long life, then finding ways of serving others altruistically is the answer. 4

To look at other statistics. The National Study of Mental Health and Wellbeing (NSMHW) is a component of the wider Intergenerational Health and Mental Health Study (IHMHS) funded by the Australian Government Department of Health.

- Over two in five Australians aged 16-85 years (43.7% or 8.6 million people) had experienced a mental disorder at some time in their life.
- One in five (21.4% or 4.2 million people) had a 12-month mental disorder.
- Anxiety was the most common group of 12-month mental disorders (16.8% or 3.3 million people).
- Almost two in five people (39.6%) aged 16-24 had a 12-month mental disorder.

After COVID-19, these numbers have risen. We were cut off from community and opportunities to be involved in ways that bring us true fulfilment.

I can't help but think that much of this is associated with how our society has developed, leaving a significant deficiency in purpose. People are starving for some purpose in their lives – a purpose that will get them out of bed in the morning. A purpose that will have them motivated to do something. It is a purpose that can pick them up from their despair of an empty life. A purpose that will have them jumping out of their comfort zone into the excitement zone. In addition, Gallup's research shows that a lack of purpose contributes to workplace dissatisfaction and disengagement.

In Melbourne, where I live, we had one of the harshest lockdowns of the COVID-19 pandemic. We were confined to travelling just within five kilometres of our homes for months on several occasions. We were not allowed to see family and friends, only able to leave our homes for the essentials. Many people fell into despair and depression that we have yet to see the full effects of. I was not immune to this.

I curled up on my couch, diving deep into self-pity one day, reliving all my past feelings of loneliness and despair. It took me back. It reminded me of the time when I was lonely, so very lonely. How could it be? I was so disconnected from everyone. I didn't feel like there was anyone else in my world. I sat day after day, talking with no one.

Without conversation. Without connection. Without community.

But there were people, people around me. There was my husband and my children. But still, my heart longed for something. It didn't know what. Life felt so empty, so meaningless. How do I fill it and refuel my life with purpose and meaning?

No, it is all too hard. There was nothing left. I couldn't see the light of day. I couldn't see that there was anything worth me getting up for.

So, I just lay there, motionless, lifeless, curled up in my bed, in a fetal position.

It was not that long before my life was filled with busyness. It was filled with friends. We laughed, we cried, we worked together, we studied together. We had deep and meaningful conversations about all sorts of things. We also had a lot of silliness that helped get us through when things got tough.

But now, here I was. Not able to get up out of bed. I couldn't even go to the shop to buy food for my family without having a major breakdown.

I had just finished four and a half years of study. Now what? I had to get out in the world and make something happen.

Nooooo! I can't do that. Too hard. No, I'll just stay here in bed.

I didn't feel safe. I was afraid of the world out there.

One day, I did pick myself up. I had to get out of this. I knew what it was. After all, I had just spent four and a half years studying Naturopathy.

My education had told me I had to get up. I had to get dressed. I had to get out in the fresh air and exercise. A walk would do to start with. I needed to ensure that I had the nourishing food to sustain me.

I knew I needed to start connecting with people.

People. Really? That's hard. That's not natural for me. I am an introvert.

Bit by bit, I started to reach out. I found a group of beautiful ladies I could connect with. It was slow, but I knew I couldn't give up. "Don't just go once. Go three or four times. You can do it. You need to do this," I told myself.

I started to find community. I joined groups where I could connect with others. It helped.

I reached out to a friend who had bought a health food shop, and I spent an unpaid day each week helping him in the shop.

Bit by bit, I started to find myself again.

It wasn't until I started to serve my communities that I could begin to feel like myself again. I forgot about my sense of loneliness. I forgot about my worries. I was now focused on others. How could I serve? How could I help them? This is where I started to discover who I am. I began to see my strengths. I began to see that I was a person of value. I had so much more to give to the world.

Here is where I started to find a greater sense of purpose. I felt like what I was doing mattered. I felt like I mattered. It was only from digging in deep, getting myself up and moving to help someone else, doing something of value for society, and giving of myself that I could get up and out of this desperate space.

I now think I might be a little bit addicted to volunteering and serving, but it makes my light shine to be able to give to others. It has given my life purpose – a **Compassionate Purpose**.

When we turn our eyes to what we can do for others, it does more than help someone else and improve the world. It makes your world, your inner world, a better place. When you contribute to society, you feel that you are someone of worth, you have something to offer, and feel good about yourself, which is reflected in everything you do.

GIVING HEALS

> *"We make a living by what we get,
> But we make a life by what we give."*
>
> *— Winston Churchill*

This quote by Winston Churchill inspired Dr Arun Dhir, a Senior Lecturer and a Specialist in Upper Gastro-Intestinal and Bariatric Surgeon. He took it to heart and developed a deep commitment to charity and being of service. He could see that there are direct health benefits in giving.

I spoke to Dr Arun on my podcast.

As a health professional, Arun dived into the research and found that people who give selflessly, more importantly, people who give to strangers, enjoy the best cardiovascular health. Studies also show that volunteers working in hospitals and other organisations had the lowest rate of heart attacks and significant instances associated with high blood pressure.

There are studies in several shapes and forms from different universities. One fascinating study looked at the science of the benefits behind giving selflessly.

In that study, university students were given $20 to spend on anything. After that experience, they measure their serum cortisol levels, which is our stress hormone. They found that the lowest stress hormone was for people who gave that $20 or bought something out of the $20 for a stranger. What this showed was that giving selflessly is beneficial for our health and wellbeing.

"I realised that the quickest way to get happy is to make others happy," shared Dr Arun.

www.SocialMissionRevolution.com/Dr-Arun-Dhir

Steve Cole at the University of California, Los Angeles, and APS Fellow Barbara Fredrickson at the University of North Carolina at Chapel Hill studied happy people. They found that people who were happy because they lived "the good life," having everything they wanted for themselves, have high levels of inflammation. (Inflammation leads to a variety of diseases, including cancer.) However, those who were happy had low inflammation because they had meaning and purpose in their lives, focusing on others with compassion and altruism.

What do you choose?

It is all about you. When you give selflessly to others, you are energised, alive, and at your best.

Chapter 4

Beyond the Why

The light flickering through the elm tree, filtering into my home office window, had me mesmerised. My mind twisted and turned like the bright green leaves in the gentle breeze on a summer morning. My large office window frames the magnificence of the tree. It was time for a Christmas message of peace, hope and love. I was waiting for that moment of inspiration.

I held a warm mug in my hands. The soothing feeling that all was right with the world engulfed me. I was sipping my tea and taking a moment to enjoy a chocolate break. As the chocolate melted divinely in my mouth, my senses were filled.

I was ready to let my thoughts go and listen to the words beyond words that would flow before me on my computer screen. I was ready for the seed of inspiration to be planted. This was a moment before a moment that would change my life and my direction.

Time to start writing. Facebook caught my attention. Before me the unthinkable was happening. There was a flurry of activity filled with uncertainty, fear and disbelief. Quickly I tuned into ABC news to see if there was truth in what was filling the newsfeed. My moment of everything feeling right with the world was turned upside down.

People at the Lindt Chocolate Café in Sydney were doing just what I was doing—taking their morning break. They were selecting the perfect chocolate, picking up their favourite brew or sitting down to converse with a friend. They were enjoying life's simple pleasures, which we take for granted. The last thing they expected was to have this moment of contentment snatched away from them by a gunman taking them hostage.

The gunman was a tall, dark-haired, and bearded man. He carried a Jihadist flag and wore a black headband with the words embossed in Arabic "We are ready to sacrifice for you, O Mohammad." He claimed that this was an attack on Australia by Islamic State.

I was glued to the news. This couldn't be true. While it was 860 kilometres from my home in Melbourne, it felt all too close to home. Only a few months before, I had been to Sydney and visited this café. I could visualise the surroundings; the sweet aroma of chocolate infused with the brewing of coffee came back to me—the glass cabinets filled with delights of chocolates and cakes. The sense of the smooth molten chocolate served up to me makes a luscious hot chocolate experience. The whole picture was alive to me.

The day seemed to drag as I stayed glued to the news reports. The momentary joy that came when three hostages escaped in the afternoon. Then another two soon after. The reality set in that this would go on so much longer.

In the early hours of the morning, a shot rang out. The gunman had shot and killed one of the hostages. Police stormed in, shooting the gunman, and an innocent hostage was hit and died.

In the aftermath, we collectively held our breath. What would happen? Would there be retaliation against the Muslim community who had nothing to do with this? The gunman was Muslim. He tried to make this look like it was a terrorist act in the name of ISIL. However, the reality was that he was a disturbed man with a criminal record who constantly sought recognition.

At the time, the community didn't know this. They just knew a Muslim, acting as a terrorist, was threatening our way of life. Would they take it out on the Muslim community?

Some of the Muslim community were afraid. They didn't want to leave their homes. If they had to, they removed their religious garb; otherwise, they thought it was like wearing a target on their head.

I could never fully understand what it must have been like for them. Every time something went wrong, since September 11, 2001, when the Twin Towers in New York were hit by planes, somehow Muslims were blamed for everything. Now we had an event on our soil. How would Australians react?

Something did happen—something beyond our expectations. A slow, quiet roar erupted on social media with #IWillRideWithYou. It appeared everywhere. People offered to ride the bus, train, and ferry with any Muslim who wasn't feeling safe to ensure they made it to their destination. Over 150,000 people made their voice heard. This country will not bow down to hate and terror but will rise in love and peace.

As I watched this appearing all over social media, the tears welled up within me. While I was saddened and shocked by what had happened in the café, my heart was filled with joy at the outpouring of love. This is the Australia that I believe in. This is the Australia I want to live in; a community accepting people for who they are, regardless of their religion, colour or place of origin. I will never forget the accounts of these two days, 15 and 16 December 2015.

I had my message of hope and love.

Thoughts of Chocolate and Coffee echoed through me over the next several months. I watched for signs that something in the world had shifted. Where was the growing community cohesiveness? Were people being more accepting of others who aren't like them?

It was early October 2016 when I had my daily chat with my Mum on the phone. I asked her, "When is Chocolate and Coffee Day?"

"I've never heard of it," she replied

"Oh, that's right, I have to start this."

Have you had one of those moments when you suddenly realise that if something is going to happen, it is up to you? You are the chosen one. Part of me wished someone else had seen this beautiful connection and possibilities. Now it was up to me.

I had no idea what I was doing. I started flooding my social media accounts with Chocolate and Coffee Day for Religious Harmony. The idea was simple and allowed everyone to be able to participate. Just reach out to someone different to you and share in chocolate, coffee and conversation.

Share in the experience of Chocolate and Coffee on 15 December. Take time at your workplace or with friends and discuss how you can be more inclusive in your community.

Chocolate, coffee and conversation. What a delicious way to change the world. The combination of chocolate and coffee is so magical.

It fills our senses and allows us to open up to someone in a comfortable environment. It is something that transcends all cultures and religions. It is something we all do. We do it to connect with our friends and family. We do it to build new relationships, whether they are personal or business. "Let's have a coffee and talk about that." It's a common phrase. It works.

Arthur Aron, a research psychologist at Stony Point University in New York, conducted studies that proved that if you listen to someone for just one hour, those terrible differences melt away. Not just to one person but the whole social group.

How powerful is that? Add the chocolate and coffee, and you have an experience filled with the joy of sharing, being opened up by the endorphins of chocolate and the warmth of your favourite brew.

Since 2016 Chocolate and Coffee Day for Religious Harmony has been held in various places and ways. From schools, workplaces, retirement villages, churches, homes, cafes, to online on Zoom and anywhere people can gather.

People have connected with me and shared how they were sharing Chocolate and Coffee Day. It brought me immense joy when I was told that a Jewish couple had invited a Palestinian on 15th December to have a conversation about peace in Israel over Chocolate and Coffee. Anything is possible.

The inevitable question came. Why is it just Chocolate and Coffee Day? There are many other times when chocolate and coffee could break down barriers.

So, Chocolate and Coffee Breaks was born. This simple idea now had a direction of its own. It can create and grow a community where there was division and isolation before.

People sharing these magic moments create an atmosphere of acceptance, inviting others to find a place where they belong. When we find belonging, we naturally want to start contributing to this new community that makes us feel at home.

It happened out of the blue. I didn't expect it; I wasn't looking for it. While looking for purpose and a way to fulfil my life, founding a social mission wasn't on my radar.

I had spent a lot of time looking at my strengths, values, and stories to find my purpose. "Start with why," Simon Sinek says. So, I searched for my why. I pieced together things that were important to me, but how could I have ever foreseen this? It is **Beyond the Why**.

I have never been the victim of prejudice. I am a white Christian woman living in Australia who was raised in the

White Australia Policy Era. Discrimination certainly wasn't at the forefront of my mind.

When we are focused on our stories and experiences, we can often miss that something that will take us beyond our imaginations. Letting go of our agendas and allowing the future to guide us, we can then discover a greater sense of fulfilment and have our ultimate impact on the world.

My fascination for the social mission started growing as I recognised the changes in me since Chocolate and Coffee Day began. It opened up the way I saw the world and myself. I felt good about myself. I had something to offer the world that made a difference.

Wanting to know more about how social mission affects people, and how we do business, led me to begin the *Social Mission Revolution* podcast. Here I explore the stories and experiences of everyday people and businesses as they take up the challenge of joining the *Social Mission Revolution*.

Over four years, I have had the pleasure and privilege of speaking with some of the most inspirational people. We will look at some of their stories in the next chapter.

CHAPTER 5

Stories from the Podcast

"But what can I do? I am just one person. I can't make a big difference." These may be the words that come to you. These words are common as we set out to find our **Compassionate Purpose**. The thought of it is daunting. You may see these grand ideas that come to others with and suddenly feel insignificant. However, I can tell you that I, and probably everyone I have had on my podcast, has felt the same at some time.

Taking on a social mission doesn't have to be about doing something grand. It may be in the small things you do. We will look later at how you can find a social mission perfect for you. It will light your fire and inspire you into action. The important thing to remember is that you don't have to change the whole world single-handedly. By changing the world for one person, you change their entire world.

You will see great variety in the social missions I have chosen to share. Some of them have started as big audacious dreams, others have been small and simple ways of making in difference in someone's life.

It is helpful to look at some of the social missions others are doing, when you are considering what yours might be. They have started with an idea and felt the compulsion that this is something *I can't not do*. They have followed the calling of this **Compassionate Purpose**. Once they hear it, nothing can stop them from making it happen.

When you hear the call of your **Compassionate Purpose**, you will understand the power of *I can't not do this*.

'**Tina Murray** is a world traveller. When she arrived in Ghana, how she could make a difference was in the back of her mind. With her passion for education, she asked schools what they needed. The response was shocking. They had no water and no toilets. Without these, schools were threatened with closure. The lack of sanitation means that going to school is not safe.

In Ghana, around 14,000 children under 5 die annually from diarrhea. The reason is diarrhoea each year. About 3,000 of that number are children. This is due to the practices such as open defecation and not having good quality drinking water. Cholera, a disease rarely seen in the Western world, is a big problem. In 2014 249 people died of cholera, and there were 22,000 cases. These deaths occurred because of something as simple as not having a bathroom.

Once they reach menstruation, girls have nowhere to take care of their needs at school, so they won't go to school for one week every month. They soon drop out, as they miss so much of their education.

Tina has become so passionate about providing toilets to schools in Ghana that she has become known as Toilet Tina. She speaks to groups and organisations about this problem and supports her local Rotary Club, which helps her raise funds to build toilets and provide water to schools.

www.SocialMissionRevolution.com/Tina-Murray

Sarifa Altono Younes and Hassan Younes were on holiday to Sarifa's homeland of The Philippines when they felt the call of *I can't not do this*.

The needs of the community moved them. A widow shared her story of desperation and hungry for her children with Sarifa. She was deeply moved and promised they would never go hungry again.

Disadvantaged children and women were in desperate need. Sarifa, being orphaned herself at a young age, had focused on educating herself to create a life of opportunities. Her heart went out to others, and so the journey began.

Together, Sarifa and Hassan were committed to making a difference. They believed that education was the key to helping people out of poverty and providing opportunities, so they started an international school in the area.

The school takes in paying students, which helps to supplement scholarships for underprivileged students. This helps to bring children from all walks of life together to give them quality education and an equal chance in life.

www.SocialMissionRevolution.com/Sarifa-and-Hassan-Younes

Kevin Milstein wanted to create a legacy to honour his son Reagan after he passed away at 14. There were two things that Reagan was passionate about football (soccer) and helping people. Kevin put these together to create the Reagan Milstein Foundation (RMF).

RMF collects pre-loved and unused sports gear and delivers it to less fortunate communities worldwide and closer to home.

Season after season, growing children need new boots and uniforms. RMF collects these from clubs and individuals and redistributes them to those in less fortunate circumstances. When they go to developing countries, it helps young people to be able to participate in sports and learn what it means to work as a team.

The Foundation has allowed Kevin to travel the world and see how sports, in general, can connect people. "It's just so important that you've got a kid who's handed in a pair of old boots, and then eventually they end up in Kenya, and somebody takes a photo of those boots with a kid in Kenya. And hopefully, the family's watching on Facebook or Twitter, and they can see that their pair of boots are connected to a kid in Kenya. In countries far less privileged than we are, an old pair of boots is like gold falling from the sky. You just don't realise how important that is."

www.SocialMissionRevolution.com/Kevin-Milstein

Randa Haverliah is the founder of Autism Mates. She is a passionate advocate and voice for those living on the Spectrum.

Autism Mates is a registered charity that exists to empower those with autism. It runs events where they have the opportunity to shine, whether it be on stage, on the catwalk or within the community. The events also allow others to volunteer and use their skills to make it possible. After all, what would a fashion show be without hairdressers and make-up artists?

Randa's son, Richard, who has autism, has been the inspiration. With the early prognosis that he would never talk, he is now a public speaker sharing the message of inclusion in schools and the community. Through his message, he helps to break down the stigma of autism, allowing us to recognise the ability that everyone has to contribute to society.

Everything Randa speaks about is not pitying seeking; it's about empowerment, "Whether I'm empowering our young people or empowering businesses to do better and to embrace their passion and their social cause."

www.SocialMissionRevolution.com/Randa-Haverliah

Karen Palmer is called the Queen of Kindness, the founder of a Global Kindness movement.

As a survivor of generational domestic abuse, Karen broke the cycle to provide her daughter with a happy and healthy home. It fuelled her passion for kindness, wanting every child to have a healthy relationship at home and at school to feel safe, heard and validated. When we do, we break the cycle of violence.

Sharing news of people doing good in the world is Karen's way of encouraging others to participate in her movement. "You start where you are, and it ripples out. That's what it's all about. Sharing kindness is about being kind to one person or to one animal at a time. Take time to be mindful and present with each person we're speaking to, with each project we're inspired by, and bring that into our community. The more we speak and act with kindness and compassion, the more it spreads worldwide. They are not random acts of kindness but intentional acts of kindness."

As a kindness educator, Karen goes into schools to teach children how they can be kind to each other. She is also a Kindness Ambassador for her home city.

www.SocialMissionRevolution.com/Karen-Palmer

Sommer Joy Ramer lives for compassion. Everything in her life focuses on how she can help bring peace to the world. In partnership with her husband, Jon Ramer, she founded Compassion Games International, a year-round non-profit initiative.

Compassion Games offers fun and creative ways to ignite and catalyse compassionate action in communities worldwide. In the annual Compassion Games, competition becomes "co-opetition" as teams and individuals challenge one another to strive together to make our planet a better place to live through community service, acts of kindness, and raising monies for local causes. The Games amplify what is already working in our communities and inspire increased engagement, leading to new activities that bring compassion to life and improve our well-being.

Players can be individuals or communities encouraged to perform random acts of kindness. These are recorded on the Compassion Games website. The impact they have made can then be seen on a map of compassion. This reports how many volunteers, hours of service, people, animals or oceans served and how much money has been donated. The collective results inspire us to do more the following year to make a more significant difference in the world.

www.SocialMissionRevolution.com/Sommer-Joy-Ramer

Robert Akeroyd was deeply touched when a Norwegian freighter ship picked up 400 asylum seekers in Australian waters. He felt deep shame when they sat on the ship for days as the Australian Government decided what to do with them. They were sent offshore for processing and detention. Their new home was prison-like camps with poor conditions; most were left there for years.

Robert wanted to do something to help these refugees feel welcome. He came up with the idea of running monthly picnics and called it "Land of Welcome." Refugees and Australian citizens come together and share a meal. "Friendships can be made when people focus on what they have in common and what unites us."

Robert has built a community where everyone belongs and benefits. People are flourishing, whether refugees or volunteers. They are given opportunities to work together and provide various types of support that are required.

Volunteers are essential in the Land of Welcome. They are trained and given roles that suit their skills and expertise. It is a growing organisation with new programs expanding throughout Australia.

https://SocialMisssionRevolution/Robert-Akeroyd

Shannon Hurley has a passion that would terrify most of us — the puppy dogs of the sea - SHARKS. (Well, some of the species are puppy dogs.) After her experiences with swimming with the sharks, she started to see them in a new light.

Shannon took her dream trip to the Galapagos Islands, where she could swim with hammerhead sharks. Her experience of swimming with these prehistoric creatures was magical.

Not long after she returned home, she was scrolling through her phone when she came across a photo that shocked her—a beautiful hammerhead shark with a hook through its eye. The article revealed that up to 90% of hammerhead sharks had been fished from the Great Barrier Reef, in Australia, in the last 50 years.

Shannon recognised the plight of sharks around the world and the critical role they play in the health of our oceans. At this moment, she knew she had to stand up and do something. There was much more at stake than the sharks. Whole food webs are becoming out of balance with dire consequences.

As a shark advocate, Shannon asks us to look at what seafood we buy to ensure that it comes from sustainable sources.

https://SocialMissionRevoultion.com/Shannon-Hurley

Sean Bell has turned a devasting moment into a message and thirst to make a difference. When he was 18 years old, one of his mates unexpectedly passed away for unknown reasons. What he took away from this was that every day could be your last day. It became essential to him to make sure that he lived his best life, with people he loves, doing things he loves. His message is, "Chase your dreams today and be the best you can."

When Sean took up marathon running, he discovered how much he loved it. Then he put a purpose to his running and fell in love with it even more. It now had a purpose greater than himself. In honour of his friend, he ran 50 marathons in 50 days, raising funds for charity.

When I spoke with Sean on the podcast, he planned to run around Australia, 14,000 km – Run for Wishes. He was training himself and building his support team. The charity, *Make a Wish Foundation*, was chosen as it aligns with his message. They help children with life-threatening illnesses get their wishes.

When COVID-19 hit, Sean's run was postponed. In April – June 2022, Sean hit the road again. He ran from Cairns to Melbourne in 60 days, raising over $100,000 for the Make a Wish Foundation.

www.SocialMissionRevolution.com/Sean-Bell

Bianca Cefalo had a dream as a child to become an engineer, not just any engineer, a rocket scientist. Yet, being a girl from a humble southern Italian family who didn't have higher education made that look unlikely. This was something that most young girls wouldn't think they could achieve. It was a difficult path because of her social and cultural conditioning. However, because of her determination, she worked hard, got her education and entered a male-dominated field.

Bianca accidentally came into her social mission when school students visited her workplace to encourage their interest in the field of science. She noticed a girl amongst all the boys, who was very intrigued by what she saw, yet seemed a little frightened. Bianca approached her. She said she was feeling out of place and that as much as the girl wanted to do this, she couldn't see that it was possible for her. Why even go to university?

At the end of the conversation, the girl felt like she could do this and go to university to study physics. This became Bianca's mission to encourage young people, especially girls, to step up and be everything they want. Don't let what appears to be an obstacle get in your way.

Bianca volunteers to speak to young people at schools and universities, sharing her story and encouraging them to take their place in the world and do what brings them joy.

www.SocialMissionRevolution.com/Bianca-Celafo

Warren Tate, like most of us, found the enforced lockdowns of the pandemic hard. His home city, Melbourne, was hit with the harshest and multiple extended lockdowns. People were isolated from family and friends for months, not allowed to leave home except for the bare essentials. While the COVID-19 numbers were going down, the numbers of people suffering from depression were going up. The suicide numbers were rising. In the midst of this, Warren started the #CallaFriendToday campaign.

Encouraging others to call friends and family during this time was important. We needed to stay connected and feel a part of a greater community. We needed to maintain stronger and deeper connections because the statistics don't lie.

Most people know of someone who has taken their life or may even be contemplating it. If we take time to communicate more effectively with others, we may save a life, save a marriage, or you could help children grow up to be better individuals. What would it mean to someone that you reached out to them and told them how amazing they are and what it is that they do matters?

Making just one phone call a day, making that connection, can make a difference.

www.SocialMissionRevolution.com/Warren-Tate

Melinda Shelley was shocked to learn that her neighbouring suburb is one of the most disadvantaged communities in Victoria. Every second child is vulnerable or at risk. She was concerned about the impact that this would have on children and their futures. Parents struggling to put food on the table can't provide books for their children. Without books, children don't learn, don't explore their full imagination and don't achieve their potential.

She heard about someone who had started a free book shop overseas and decided she could do something to help these children succeed by giving them books. The owner of a thrift shop in the area was happy to have a cardboard box of free books for children to take home in her store. Melinda would go back every week and refill the box.

Melinda's commitment to improving the lives of local disadvantaged children was the beginning of 123Read2Me, a charity that has donated over 600,000 free books to underprivileged children all over Australia.

Melinda's goal is to empower kids to succeed with free books. International research is overwhelming; we know when children have access to books and someone to read to them every day, they will have more words to use in their day-to-day, and this creates an ability to think, question, and imagine, which leads to an ability to solve problems which makes a better life.

www.SocialMissionRevolution.com/Melinda-Shelley

Peter Nicholls went with his daughter on her Year 9 school trip to Papua New Guinea (PNG). At the end of Kokoda Track, they arrived at a village. They discovered a school. It had two or three classrooms and incomplete teachers' quarters. Even though they had been given money as compensation after the war, it wasn't enough to finish the work.

He returned to Australia and put his skills in theatre to use with a fundraising concert. Peter returned to help the locals complete the school. Now they had a school with good facilities, children and teachers wanted to be there.

Peter's eyes were now opened to the needs of people in countries such as PNG. He became overwhelmed with trying to help them all. "I realised I didn't need to change the world. I just needed to change the one, just one at a time. There's one act of kindness at a time because just doing that one good deed has a ripple effect." And so, his charity *Change the One* began with a focus on helping one person or community at a time.

After a holiday to Vietnam, he found more schools that needed help and returned several times to help build schools. *Change the One* has also been helping those with disabilities caused by Agent Orange.

www.SocialMissionRevolution.com/Peter-Nicholls

Alan Stevens is a Profiling and Communications Specialist. He teaches others how to read people. In his work, he found that men had become confused about their role in the family and society. They had grown up in a world where they were told that, as the man, they were the breadwinner. With the rise of feminism, political correctness and the #MeToo movements, they are no longer sure how they should behave around women. Their whole sense of who they were was being questioned.

These are things that men generally aren't comfortable talking about. Seeing the frustrations and where these led men, Alan set out to create a safe place for men to open up and talk about these topics.

Alan created The Campfire Project, where men could unite, build relationships, and share their stories. They discuss topics such as femininity, masculinity, pornography, drugs, alcohol, etc. Alan puts together panel discussions with experts for more in-depth understanding.

Women are always welcome; he feels it is essential that they hear what men think and feel. #WeTogether is the emphasis, encouraging men and women to work together.

From a small beginning, The Campfire Project is now a global community where now both men and women come together to share their stories and join in respectful conversations through the power of social media. www.SocialMissionRevolution.com/Alan-Stevens

Scott Carson, his wife and his two-year-old son went on a bike ride. It was a perfect day until his wife came off her bike. There she was, lying motionless on the ground, blood pouring out of her. Scott cradled her head while managing a screaming toddler. Everyone kept walking and driving past. No one stopped to help.

His wife learned to walk and talk again and is doing well. However, it freaked Scott out that nobody would stop. It burned a massive hole in him. So, he thought, what's the one thing he could do to change how we are, to bring people back to caring about each other? He realised that to have conversations and support each other, we needed to rebuild trust first. He took it upon himself to find a way to change this. He went into the business of smiles.

To reconnect with the community, Scott takes time to stop and talk to people. He gives them a pair of bright yellow socks with black polka dots. "The black dots represent our dark days. We all have them no one's getting out of that. The yellow is the warm winter sun on your back. And a smiley face. There are times of darkness, but there is always so much more sun." He thanks them for doing their best.

Through connecting with people and making them smile, Scott is helping to bridge the gap of separation that stops people from caring for others in the community. www.SocialMissionRevolution.com/Scott-Carson

Alex Dekker offered to make his sister a meal to help her during the COVID-19 lockdowns in Melbourne. As a frontline working in the first COVID hospital ward, her time and energy for preparing nutritious meals was limited.

While he was at it, he might as well provide for others who needed it. He went on to Facebook and offered his networks something to eat. About 400 people requested a simple meal. He wasn't expecting this response.

He had no idea what he was doing. He had no skills or resources in this area, but he thought he would give it a go. He sought assistance from friends and cold-called companies, restaurants and chefs to help. A week later, he sent out 800 meals.

The need continued right through the extended COVID lockdowns in Melbourne. After the lockdowns ended, his services have continued with his commitment to providing quality and nutritious meals that respect the dignity of those in need.

Alex Makes Meals now sends out 800 meals daily through various charities around Victoria. The charities are working on the frontline with people in desperate need. Providing these meals allows the charity to focus on what they do best, helping people.

Alex Dekker is the 2022 Victorian Young Australian of the Year.   www.SocialMissionRevolution.com/Alex-Dekker

Vera Entwistle was grieving her father's death when she read an article to read about a 10-year-old girl, Teddy and her family. This girl had cancer, and the article told how she and her family were dealing with it. It touched Vera's heart and left her wondering if they had a secret that would help her deal with her pain.

She reached out to them and discovered they took their daughter on a camp along with 12 other children who had cancer and did the things other kids take for granted. This lifted her spirits along with all those who went.

Vera was about to move to Australia from the USA and promised that when she arrived, she would volunteer at a similar camp. There were no such programs. Determined that this was a good idea, Vera started Camp Quality, a program of camps and support for children with cancer.

Children come along to camp and have fun being kids. They have an adult companion who ensures that each one gets all the support they need to enjoy every moment of the camp. The companion continues to support the child and their family after the camp. This helps the children deal with the long, arduous journey of coping with cancer treatments.

On the podcast Vera talked about the difficult journey of getting Camp Quality started. There was a lot of negativity from others, who kept telling her that it wouldn't work. However, from talking with the children who were cancer patients, she knew that this was needed. They wanted it. It would give them hope and something to look forward to.

Vera listened to her gut instinct which told her that this would work. She was not going to give in. Camp Quality will be celebrating 40 years of camps in 2023.

Vera's advice for you is that if you have an idea that your gut tells you, this is really going to be a winner. Put the blinders on and go for it. Don't listen to the negativity, and don't let anybody discourage you from starting.

www.SocialMissionRevoultion.com/Vera-Entwistle

These are just some of the stories from the *Social Mission Revolution* podcasts. Please take time to listen to them. The guests tell their stories with a truly inspirational passion. Each one also gives some advice to help you on your journey of becoming a Social Mission Revolutionist.

Each of these stories gives you a glimpse into various ways of making a difference in the world. Maybe something you read captured your imagination and sparked an idea of what you may like to do.

Becoming involved in a social mission can be looked at in various ways. On the podcast, my eyes have been opened to many more opportunities for us to be involved. It can be as simple as looking at the businesses we support and buying our goods and services. I speak about some of these in my book *Compassionate Prosperity – When Success is Not Enough*.

- Make conscious choices around where we buy our clothing. Is it manufacturing slave-free?
- Are the products we use environmentally friendly?
- Do we recycle and reduce waste in our homes and businesses?
- Do the services we choose support our values, and are they consciously involved in social mission?

Becoming a Social Mission Revolutionist can challenge us in many ways. You don't have to do everything at once. What is it that speaks to you? Start there.

There is no hard and fast rule about what your social mission should or could look like. You may have an idea of something that can be taken to the world in a big way. Or you might have something you can do for someone who lives next door.

On the podcast with **Lillian Brummet**, we talked about some simple ways people can serve and get involved in social missions.

Lillian told the story of an elderly lady who lived in her neighbourhood as a teenager. This lady inspired her on her path as a Social Mission Revolutionist. The neighbour turned her front yard into a flower garden. The blooms were then taken to an elderly citizen's home, a hospital, palliative care and a church.

It was something so simple that this lady could do. She brought smiles and happiness to others in their times of need by doing what she loved—growing a garden of flowers.

www.SocialMissionRevolution.com/Lillian-Brummet

Whatever your skills and talents are, there is something you can do wherever you are in life.

Take a look at your life with new eyes. How can something that you love to do transform into a social mission?

Chapter 6

The Languages of Social Mission

Curiosity took hold of me. Why did my social mission evolve the way it did? Chocolate and Coffee Breaks is all about sitting down with someone, touching their lives, learning about each other, and recognising and acknowledging each other. At the same time, other people take up causes that evolve entirely differently. They may raise lots of money. They may knit blankets for the sick or homeless or make cute little joey pouches. They might take care of those joeys. Or, for them, it might be about doing those behind-the-scenes jobs that have to be done. There is a whole gamut of different ways to express a social mission. Why this one?

There are three sisters. Whenever I think about giving styles, I think of them. Their sameness of spirit is evident. They are compassionate women with giving hearts, yet the way they express giving is so different.

Louise creates and writes beautiful messages to people. She encourages them to keep on going when things get tough. She supports them through their journey with the gift of words. It is always something exceptional to receive a card in the mail from Louise. They mean so much to everyone she has touched in this way.

Mary has the gift of service. You will find her in the kitchen at any event or gathering, ensuring everything is taken care of. She will see what needs to be done and do it. It also brings her great pleasure to spend the day in her kitchen making jams and preserves that can be sold for fundraisers.

Joan is someone different again. When I think of her, I feel her presence. She loves being with people, talking, and listening to them. While she will also offer service and words, her natural gift is how people feel heard when they are with her.

We all have different styles. When I look at the people I have spoken to on the *Social Mission Revolution* podcast and their different ways of expressing their social mission. I see them come alive.

This is such an essential aspect for us to look at. Most books, ideas and suggestions around altruism and philanthropy focus on the concept of fundraising and giving money. While I appreciate that all social missions can benefit from cash injections, if this is not your giving style, it could leave you feeling empty and having to do more. Of course, I do encourage all to give where they can because, let's face it, no matter what the social mission is, at some stage, it needs money to grow and develop. However, we are looking for a social mission that feels genuine and fulfilling to you.

My primary Love Language is physical touch. In this new era of COVID times, touch isn't something we can give or receive a lot. When I explored how I feel when I share my social mission and what is important, it came to me that it is about a greater sense of touch. When I feel that I am touching someone's life, touching them on an emotional or spiritual level, I feel that I am giving. It is all about giving them the feeling that someone is there with them.

My secondary Love Language is quality time, which is evident in the concept of Chocolate and Coffee Breaks. It's all about giving time and holding the space to be present with someone. I can do the other languages, but I find my greatest sense of fulfilment when I do these. I do it naturally and with ease and make the most significant impact.

When I look at how I volunteer and what I volunteer for, I see how this resonates with me. One of my volunteer gigs is as a Community Chaplin in the Victoria Council of Churches Emergency Ministries (VCCM). Here my role is to be with people in times of need. We are deployed to support the community when there is an emergency, such as bushfires, floods, storms or tragedies. We listen to people. We hold space for them to come to terms with the situation and grieve when needed. We create calm in the middle of chaos. Here is where my Love Language speaks. I may not physically touch them, but I am touching them by holding space and giving them quality time.

What is your giving style? These are based on the *5 Love Languages* by Dr Gary Chapman. In his many years of experience as a marriage counsellor, he found that there are five languages.

We all have one or sometimes two ways to prefer to be loved and love. We don't feel loved if we don't experience this type of love. In return, the way we express love is in our Love Language. All is good if our loved ones speak the same language. If they don't, it takes a lot of love and understanding to make it work. You can quickly feel unloved by someone who loves you deeply just because they don't express love the way you need it.

If the way we express our social mission aligns with our Love Language, or as I call it, our Giving Style, then we will be able to expend much more energy in our giving, as it will energise us.

The five Love Languages are

- Acts of Service
- Gifts
- Words of Affirmation
- Quality Time
- Physical Touch

Acts of Service

The way you express love is to serve. The saying "actions speak louder than words" rings true to you. Your way of expressing love is to take care of someone's needs. You feel love when someone does something for you that may make your life easier. Many people I have spoken to on the *Social Mission Revolution* have Acts of Service as their primary language. They feel a need to serve, so they will find a way to help others in a physical sense. In serving, they feel complete.

My husband's primary Love Language is Acts of Service. When I spoke to him about the different styles of giving in social mission and told him that some people work at earning more money, spending less so that they can provide more, he felt that was a "cop-out." While he can be extremely generous, he needs to be physically serving in some way to feel that he is making a difference.

These people are often easy to pick out. They are always in the kitchen at parties. They have to help.

Words of Affirmation

The way you express love is through words. Hearing genuine words of encouragement and appreciation is essential to you and makes you feel loved. Your way of expressing love is to give verbal or written praise. Saying those words "I love you" is so important. Of course, you also love to hear them. You will feel loved when you do. You love to get notes and messages filled with feelings, support, appreciation and recognition.

Regarding social mission, I have found that for people who have the Love Language of Words of Affirmation, it is not necessarily the words. It is the affirmation that what they are doing is making a difference.

It may be a smile or the laughter of children they have helped. Seeing photos or statistics of what they have done makes it all worthwhile.

Those with Words of Affirmation may be writing letters to seek changes in the words. They find a way to use their voice to advocate for others.

Of course, words of recognition for what they have done never go astray.

Giving Gifts

The way you feel loved is by receiving gifts. You express your love by giving meaningful gifts and a reflection of your relationship with the giver. You always find that perfect gift. It gives you so much pleasure to find that special something. You always have something on hand to offer. You feel loved when you receive a gift. It makes you feel special and thought of.

Regarding social mission, those with Giving Gifts may find contentment in giving money. However, there are many people I have spoken to who want to put the time and effort into selecting the perfect gift or way to give money.

In *Compassionate Prosperity*, one of the businesses I highlighted was The Hope Initiative. From every sale they make, a percentage goes to charity. However, Cascie Kambouris doesn't give them cash. She finds out what items a required and physically goes out to buy them.

The Love Language of Giving Gifts is about making sure that a meaningful gift is given.

Quality Time

The way you express love is through spending time with people. It doesn't matter how busy you are. You are never too busy to sit and be with someone. You will give your time freely. You feel loved when others spend quality time with you. Nothing says "I love you" more than someone making time to be with you. It is not about quantity but that undivided time when you can focus on each other. It is about being present with someone.

Someone with the Love Language of Quality Time wants their time to be well spent. It must have a purpose.

They will happily give their time to sit and listen to someone in their time of need. As long as it takes, they are there.

You often find a Quality Time person working with a group of people and supporting and empowering them.

Time is a precious commodity. A person with the love language of time will freely give their time to someone in need. However, it is essential that their time is used in a valuable way and not wasted.

Physical Touch

You express love by reaching out and touching another person. It may just be a touch of the hand or a hug. You naturally touch others in conversation. To feel loved, you need physical contact. Nothing says "I love you" more than a hug.

Physical Touch people are often involved in activities such as massage or physical healing arts. They are happy to give and receive this gift.

There are many ways touch can be used that we don't immediately think of. What can you touch? A hand or a cup as you pass it to someone. You can pat an animal or hold a child. You can craft something with your hands.

Physical touch can be a little trickier in a social mission, especially in COVID times. However, as this is mine, I could feel what is most important to me. I need to feel that I have "touched" someone's life and created a connection with them. The emotional or spiritual touch is just as important and valid for those with the gift of touch-to-touch lives.

An example of this is my social mission – Chocolate and Coffee Breaks which also represents my secondary love language of giving quality time.

Our Giving Styles can be a mix of these. As your giving style relates directly to your Love Language, the easiest way to find your Love Language is to go to https://www.5lovelanguages.com and do the quiz which will give you your Love Language.

How you express your social mission will become more apparent when you understand your giving style. It will feel natural and easy for you. The chances are that you will automatically do this. What is important here in recognising your style is knowing that however you choose to express your social mission, it is perfect.

The value I see in looking at your Love Languages when looking at your social mission is ensuring that you are doing something that will fill you up and energise you. While there are skills you can offer, they will drain you if they are in the wrong setting. For example, I can offer my administrative or organisation skills to a cause. However, if I'm stuck in the back room by myself, with my Love Languages of Physical Touch and Quality Time, I feel like I'm wasting my most valuable asset – touching people's lives.

We don't all have to raise a million dollars. We don't all have to take on massive projects. If what speaks to your heart is something that touches one person at a time, then that is great in my eyes. I have what I have set out to do.

Chapter 7

Uncovering Your Ultimate Impact

Are you ready to have your life completely disrupted? Your agenda, your goals, your plans completely thrown out the window? Are you ready to discover the greatest joy and fulfilment you could ever hope to find?

Well, I have warned you.

Once you feel that passion building up, that longing to make that difference that you know you are here to make, there is no turning back. *You can't not do this.*

Maybe you've spent your life doing what everyone says you are supposed to do – earn money, get a car, buy a house, get married, and have children. You work hard, but it's never quite hitting that satisfaction spot. It is time to stop going around in circles. There is that burning question that keeps coming up.

"How can I make a difference?"

Whether you are an individual seeking this answer or want your business to have that ultimate impact, a legacy that you can live and be proud of, it is time to dig deep and find how you can unleash your ultimate impact on the world.

But how do we make a difference? How do we find something that calls to us, that gives us that passion and drive to step up and out of our comfort zones to make something happen?

This took a lot of work for me. I have spent much time alone, in my home, working away, behind my computer. Very comfy! My first business was about how I could do what I'd just spent years training to do without going out of my comfort zone.

As an introvert, what I had trained to do had me sitting at the discomfort level. Sitting in an office one-on-one with people in naturopathic consultations was uncomfortable. What was I thinking? I just wanted to run and hide. So, I did. I started my business on the internet. It was all new and exciting, and I jumped into that with passion and zeal. I could do my work without leaving the comfort of my lovely cosy little world.

Then the time came when I needed more. The excitement wore off as I sat there day in, day out, packing apricot kernels. I needed to find something more, something that would sustain my excitement. I needed something that would give me the feeling that I was achieving something every day, growing, developing and, importantly, making a difference. I needed something exciting. I needed to find out how I could make my ultimate impact on the world.

We all feel we have a purpose. This gives us the direction in life we need. We search to find that deep sense of fulfilment and ask and ask and ask: "What is it I'm supposed to be doing in life?"

Then there is the why. Why is it that I'm compelled to do what I do? Why do I get out of bed each morning? Why do I feel I have to do this? This is the story we tell. The story that gets people on board helps to give us the path we are to take to get to our destination – our purpose.

But is it enough? When we go **Beyond the Why** to discover something braver, something more potent, we find the energy and passion that will drive us to our destination. We need to find the vehicle that we will use to get there.

I have done much purpose work, so I understand where my direction is. It is all about helping people find passion in purpose. Awesome. Great. Got it. Now what? That on its own wasn't enough. What do I do with this now? Who are these people? How do I do this? This is the direction where I set my GPS, but how do I get there? There are so many paths I could take and many vehicles to drive. I needed more to get me off my butt and moving.

I searched for a why. Why did I find myself moving in the direction I was going?

My why comes from my experience after selling my business and getting a "real job." I discovered that the business world felt empty and soulless. I thought about the years I spent being collateral damage as the wife and mother who had to pick up the pieces that the stress of dispassionate, soulless work leaves in ruins.

It is more than just marriages and family lives that suffer; it is society, broken lives and broken families that try to carry on in a world without comprehending the meaning. I wanted more for my children as they make their own lives in the working world, and I wanted more for me. This, for me, was the route I was to take in living out my Purpose. I had now set my GPS and had the path mapped out before me.

But I found that this was just the storyline. Yes, I felt passionate about it, but it still wasn't what was going to get me leaping out of bed with excitement each morning. I'll just turn over and go back to sleep. Everyone can sort out their problems, just as I had to.

I needed a vehicle to know how to follow this path and in which direction to take it. What would make me excited to jump out of bed when I hadn't slept for a week? What is it?

How am I to work with a **Compassionate Purpose**? How am I to make an impact? How can I have my ultimate impact?

We can't all be all things. Discovering your greatest superpower for yourself will allow you to make great strides towards achieving your ultimate impact and becoming an **Authentic Influence**. Once you have this, you have full awareness of where your excitement zone is, and you will quickly discern the projects and even jobs that will bring out your best, that you will enjoy and that you will be able to give your total commitment to.

Through this work, I have uncovered that exploring who you are and what motivates you will help to define the what, why and how you can discover what you *can't not do* and unleash your ultimate impact on the world.

Let's start exploring.

STORIES

I've shared with you the stories that have shaped my path. When I look back on them, I see them as the "way-shower." They have shed light on my path and helped me understand myself and what is most important to me.

When I work with people and explore their stories, I can start to see the threads that run through them. Sometimes there is a story deep down that we have forgotten about or seems insignificant that does point the way.

When we take time to explore, we start to remember people and places. Ask yourself, "What is the significance of this?" "How has this shaped who I am? Where am I going? Why do I do the things I do?"

Uncovering our own stories is more than finding our threads. It helps you piece together the essential pieces you can share with others.

Stories are the heartbeat of communities. They are the foundation of all cultures and societies. We need to share stories. We need to hear stories. They help us understand who we are as individuals, communities, and workplaces.

When you find the gold in your own story, you have something valuable to share as a legacy to others. So, let's dig deep.

Delve into the stories that made you who you are today.

- What are the stories that shaped you?
- What jobs have you had? The ones you have loved? The ones you have hated? What are the tasks you did that made you feel good about yourself? What didn't?
- Who influenced your life, directions, and who you are?
- What events influenced you and how?

When you start to see and identify these, the tapestry of your life will begin to reveal itself to you as you see the threads that have woven their way throughout your life.

STRENGTHS

Have you ever been in a job or volunteered to help and found yourself doing something that isn't you? You look across and see someone else struggling to do what it is that you can do so quickly you could just about do it in your sleep – such a waste of resources.

Nothing will kill your enthusiasm for what you are doing quicker than doing a role that "just isn't you." Just because you can do it doesn't mean you should or have to. Have you heard of the word "NO?"

In any position, volunteering or otherwise, there will always be a mix of things you excel at, something you enjoy, things you are good at, things you don't mind doing, and things you find difficult but look forward to the challenge. And then there are those things you'd rather not do. You know you're not good at them and have no interest in doing them, so these are going to be the tasks that are always left to last, are poorly done or remain undone.

What is vital with your social mission is that you are doing what you are good at and, most importantly, what you love. Anything else is going to be a drain on the valuable resource that is you. The idea is to inspire and motivate, not run you into the ground.

Find your Easy Power

We often don't recognise what our natural gifts are. This is because they do come easy to us. You find yourself saying, "Doesn't everyone know that?" These are the things that are important for us to take notice of. The things you think are easy and basic just aren't for everyone. The tricky thing about your easy place is recognising it. When you can focus on these "easy" things and develop your skills around them, you are in a position of easy power.

It took me 40 years of leadership roles before I realised that leadership was one of my strengths. I just hadn't thought about it – the same with speaking. I have been speaking in front of people since I was a small child. It hadn't occurred to me that I could have a gift for it.

Think about what it is that you have been doing all your life. What are those things that everyone else doesn't do? These may be your easy power. When you can step into these and use them to work on your social mission, staying in love with your mission will be easier.

Finding Your Strengths

Gallup Research found that those who know their strengths are more engaged and productive at work and three times more likely than others to have an excellent quality of life. When we know what these are, it makes a difference. We can look at a task or position and know we can make a go of it. When things don't go right the first, fifth, or twentieth time, we will keep going because we have the awareness that this is something that, once I train myself to do, I can make work.

Over the past several years, I have done a myriad of different tests and exercises and explored various modalities that help to reveal just what my strengths and purpose are. They all have shown something about me that I have taken on board. My strengths, according to Gallup, are Connectedness, Maximiser, Ideation, Realtor and Strategic. When I put these together, I do "Ideas and strategies to maximise relationships and connections." Now take a look at what my social mission is. Is this what I do? Add my strengths of leadership, speaking, organising, negotiating and community (according to Human Design), and you have what I do perfectly in alignment.

When you have identified your strengths, you will have the confidence to step up and say this is who I am and what I can do. It uncovers the talents you rely on to build relationships, think strategically, execute plans and influence others to accomplish goals.

Identifying what your natural talents are will always bring a moment of clarity.

What are the things that you find easy to do? There are many different types of strength tests available that can highlight just what your strengths are. Gallup Strength test is excellent at outlining this clearly for you.

What I have found particularly helpful is Human Design. It has helped me identify who I am, what I am here to do and who I am here to serve. While you may know deep down what your strengths are, having them set out clearly in front of you gives you permission to claim and make the most of them.

Ask those closest to you what they think you are good at. Ask a variety of people from all different walks of your life. Sometimes those who are closest to us also miss them.

Inventory your skills. Make a list of all the things you are good at. Think about your hobbies and interests. What are the things you enjoy doing? Do you like gardening, cooking, writing, or running? Whatever you can think of, write them down.

PASSIONS

I was asked to go on a committee to review a community publication. It wasn't something I felt passionate about, but I was asked, so I did. Weeks went by without hearing from any of the other members. Me being me thought, OK, I have to take the lead. I sent an email to the others – still nothing. Weeks went by. I sent out another email. Eventually, I got one response. The response was, "I don't care about this".

What had happened was that the person who had asked me had asked each of the others as well. Their thinking was about who they could get involved in "something." Not who was passionate about making a change in this area. The fact was that not one member of this committee cared about this particular project. So, nothing was done.

All I could do was send an email back to the original "inviter" and inform him that we were not interested. If you want something done, get people who have a passion for the project or task.

It is so vital that we understand our passions when it comes to our social mission. We need to be doing the things that get us excited. We need to be involved in activities that keep us motivated and enjoy doing.

Something that I am passionate about is social mission. I love talking about it. I love finding out about it. I love to immerse myself in a world where people care and do something about what they are passionate about.

One of the activities that always lights me up is leading a group through the process of developing ideas and strategies. I love the energy. I love the way ideas pop into existence. The opportunity to do this will pick me up from the darkest moment and set me on my highest energy.

We all have things that we are passionate about; these may be a sporting team, our favourite hobby, pets, etc. However, we are talking about recognising our deep-down underlying passions.

- What is it that moves and motivates you?
- What are the issues in life that get you going?
- What are the things that excite you about your work and your life?
- What drives you into action when you feel that staying in bed for the day would be a real option?

Now take a fresh look at your skills inventory. Which ones evoke a passionate response? Which ones excite you?

VALUES

Our values are so important to identify. These are the ideals that shape who you are and the decisions you make. They are the energetic drivers that we place as essential to us.

They influence our thoughts, words and actions. They shape the way we live our lives.

When we are clear on these, we can apply them to everything we do and our decisions, aligning with who we are. If you aren't clear on these, you may find them by going back through what you have already written down. Look for those common themes and threads.

If you find it difficult, Google a list of values and see which ones stand out. Compare them with the other areas you have covered in your stories, strengths and passions. Circle the ones that speak to you. There may be something completely different that comes to mind. Write that down as well. Then go through and compare each one to the next. Which one is most important to you? See if you can come up with your top three values.

ULTIMATE IMPACT

How will you have your Ultimate Impact?

With all these before you, you can see the common threads woven through your storyline. It's time to grab your coloured highlighters and find those recurring words, themes and concepts. This will give you a new list of things that make up the tapestry of your life. It is always exciting when I work with people doing this process. A sudden illumination happens when all the puzzle pieces come together.

Put these aside and take some time to allow new words and visions to unfold. This is something not to rush but to let wash over you as you take time to let go of all that was. Allow something more significant to come forward from the future by spending time in meditation or taking a walk and listening to music. Do whatever it is you do to clear your mind.

Come back to it fresh and look at who you are. What is it you do? Who is it you do it for? What is the result? This is not a "why" exercise. It is a "what and how". This is the vehicle you drive on the route set out by your why on the way to your **Compassionate Purpose**.

It may take a while to play around with words to find the right combination that speaks to you. Sit in a quiet space, connect with the feel, and create ten different statements. You will find the words that speak to you as your **Ultimate Impact Statement**.

My **Ultimate Impact Statement** is: *I guide diverse individuals to work together in community to create change.* I know that I am at my best when I am doing this. I am energised and able to do things beyond what I or anyone else thought was possible. This is what lights my fire more than anything else.

My social mission and my work, including volunteering positions, are all based on my **Ultimate Impact Statement**. Everything I do has a basis in nourishing people in community so they can be empowered as individuals and as a group. If an offer to do something doesn't fit within this, I know that I won't be fulfilling my potential if I take it on.

Once you have an **Ultimate Impact Statement** that feels right for you, go back through your skills inventory. You will have a fresh perspective on how you can use your skills in a compassionate way that will thrill and delight you.

When we understand how we can naturally and easily have our ultimate impact on the world, utilising our natural gifts and skills, we can see which things to say yes to and which ones to say no to.

If we can uncover the what, how and why we commit to this "something" and keep that in front of us, it can help us to maintain our commitment through the ups and downs.

The more you know yourself, the more ready you are to take on a social mission.

BEYOND THE WHY

Finding the social mission that will speak to your heart takes more than creating an **Ultimate Impact Statement**. It takes more than knowing your strengths, stories, passions, values and Love Language. It takes more than an understanding of your Purpose.

You need to find something new emerging calling to your heart. You may find that there isn't a why in all the logical sense of your own life. It is something greater you feel you must do for others' benefit, not yours. Here amazing things happen, and your life can be transformed along with others. It is **Beyond the Why**, and you move totally into altruistic motives. It is not for you; it is for someone else. Here you can make a real difference.

So maybe it is time for us to stop looking at ourselves and start giving of ourselves.

How do we find something that calls to us and gives us that passion and drive to step up and out of our comfort zones to make something happen?

We all have some understanding about that small still voice that speaks to us. When in your quiet moments of reflection or through a sudden spurt of inspiration, you are led into new places and new ideas.

Once you have this type of certainty, there is no turning back. You have heard your calling and have to give it your all; nothing else will do. Nothing else will provide you with a sense of fulfilment. You just have to go **Beyond the Why**. Here you have your ultimate impact on the world.

So how do we get from developing our **Ultimate Impact Statement** to having our Ultimate Impact? It takes letting go. Letting go of it all and listening.

Before we get there, I like to throw in that magic question that connects you with a glimpse of what that might be. This question is the one I ask every guest on the *Social Mission Revolution* podcast. The variations and also the sameness fascinate me.

The question is:

If there was just one thing for you to fight for, what would it be?

I was first confronted with this question many years ago, long before the thought of the *Social Mission Revolution*. I had an immediate response within me. It came to my mind that I fight for freedom of spiritual expression. It was something that had always been important to me.

I firmly believe that every person should have the right to find their spiritual path. Something always burned up inside me when I saw people persecuted for their beliefs. For some reason, **Beyond the Why**, this became the passion that haunted me.

Over the past few years, as I have grown within the *Social Mission Revolution*, I have delved deeper. With the understanding of my values and the journey I have been on, I respond a little differently when asked what I fight for.

Now my response is that I fight for the "worth of all persons." I believe everyone has the right to be treated fairly and equally. Each one deserves the right to be given the same opportunities, no matter who they are, where they are from, what they believe, or who they love.

We all have that basic human need to be accepted for who we are, to have a community where we belong and the opportunity to contribute to finding purpose and fulfilment in life. This is my passion, and it speaks through everything I do.

I ask this question of people often. It is the one question that I ask the guests on my podcast to be prepared for. Some guests find this easy to answer. Others need time to contemplate and connect to it. I love to ask this question as it is interesting to see what correlation their response has to the social mission that they have grown.

The point has often come up from these kind-hearted, peace-loving people that they are not fighters. They don't want to fight but want to put all they have into creating something for the world or solving a problem they feel called to act on.

When I talk about "fighting for something", my thoughts don't go to starting a literal war. I am talking about embracing the situation with your whole heart, mind and soul. You put yourself on the line for it. You give everything you have got. What speaks so strongly to you that you have to stand for this? Would you put yourself in the line of fire this?

One of my favourite responses came from **Shelly Galvin**, Corporate Social Responsibility Director at CBT Nuggets. This was what she said,

> "I really love it when people ask me this question, and it brings me back to a moment that I had in a course for the University for Peace, the peace which is the UN's mandated university located in San Jose, Costa Rica, and they have an Executive Education. I took a course from a professor named John Hartman called Regenerative Leadership. And in this course, he asked us, the students, "What do you think is the most pressing, the worst issue in the world today?" And we all have our own lens. There were people saying war, famine or global warming and poverty and he said, "No, that's not the biggest problem facing the world today. The biggest problem facing the world today is the human heart. If we all acted through our hearts, we wouldn't harm each other. We wouldn't harm the environment; we wouldn't harm animals. We would work together." So, for me, what would I fight for? I would fight for people to really work through their hearts."

To me, this holds up as the perfect answer. When we connect with our hearts to all, there can never be any of these other problems in the world. Maybe that is the true essence of the *Social Mission Revolution*.

WHAT IS IT THAT YOU WOULD FIGHT FOR?

You have spent some time looking at your stories, strengths and skills, values, and passions. When you start to see the threads that weave through these, the themes of your life may begin to give clues on what this thing you stand for is. If it isn't clear at first, that's OK. It may well be something that you have never considered before.

Allow yourself some time for it to come to you. Think about the issues that confront you in life. What are the situations that you are drawn to take notice of? Where do you find yourself feeling that something should be done about this? What are the circumstances that bring tears to your eyes?

It will be there when you are open to being observant of what is calling you. Don't rush it. It will come. It's also OK if it changes or morphs into something else.

IT IS TIME TO LET GO

Congratulations. You have done the work. You have explored your stories, uncovered your strengths, delved into your passions, revealed your values and discovered your giving style. You know how you can have your Ultimate Impact on the world. You have felt into the depth of your being to find what you would fight for.

Now what? You still have to find that social mission that will revolutionise your life.

Sometimes in the process, something comes to you that speaks to your heart. The important starting point is this process that allows you to discover yourself and your superpowers. When it does arrive, you know that this is it and that if you apply what you have found in your **Ultimate Impact Statement**, you will have your ultimate impact on the world.

It is commonly said, "When you are looking for love, you don't find it. It comes when it is least expected." It can be like that with a social mission. Then, you ask, "Why did we need to do all that work to start with?"

Just like finding love, the journey starts within. We need to be able to see ourselves for who we are. We need to understand what is important to us. We need to know how we are best suited to serve.

The path will be somewhat easier when we have all of that together. When you know how we are designed to give, the things you do light you up, your strengths, and you find a cause that fills your heart, you know how to serve.

You will understand how you can give yourself entirely in a way that will drive you and fuel your passion rather than drain it. Many people lose their desire to serve when they serve in the wrong way for them.

Now is the time to let go. You know the why. You know the how. You are now looking for the what.

Bringing together your **Ultimate Impact Statement** with what you fight for can open up thoughts and ideas. Looking at your stories, strengths, passions and values through the lens of your **Ultimate Impact Statement** can start the process of how you can serve in the most fulfilling way.

However, that is your mind thinking it through. When you let your heart be the guide, something powerful will come forward. Let's look at mine as an example.

If I return to my initial response of what I would fight for, then add my **Ultimate Impact Statement**, this is what emerges – "I fight for freedom of spiritual expression by guiding community in developing ideas and strategies that maximise relationships and connections."

It might seem obvious now, but before the event that set it in motion, I would not have had the powerful impetus of Chocolate, Coffee and Conversation. The form of what it could be would not have developed

Having those other two elements in place opens your senses to possibilities. You are now more consciously alert to what comes into your field. It's like when you decide to buy a particular make of car. You may have never noticed it on the road before, but as soon as you do, suddenly you see it everywhere. You are subconsciously on the watch for it.

Take some time to let these elements wash over you. Journal your feelings about what they mean. Review your stories, and write them out. Reflect on what your values mean to you.

What happens when you put your answer to "What would you fight for, with your Love Language and your **Ultimate Impact Statement**? Do you see some magic before you?

Take some time with all of this, and with no agenda. Just see the possibilities that present themselves. Write down all of the different mixes that intrigue you. They just may be a piece of brilliance.

When you are ready, it will come.

You have not chosen this path.
This path has chosen you.

Chapter 8

You Are Not Enough

I am not enough. Have you ever felt that way?

I am not enough, and I'm damn proud of it.

It was 2019 when I found myself sitting in a high school classroom for an evening meeting. The room was used primarily for Year 7 students. I looked up and saw a sign on the wall. The teacher would have put it there intending to motivate the children.

As I looked at it, I put myself in the place of a 12-year-old who would have been looking at it every day. So please imagine with me.

You read it. You read it again and again. Day after day, it is staring at you. Hmmm, what does that mean? "I may not be perfect, but I am enough."

You think of all the uses of the word "enough".

Mum asks if we've had enough to eat.

Did I do well enough on my test?

I hear Mum and Dad saying, "Do we have enough for the bills this month?"

And then there is the "I've had enough!". Yes, she definitely says that.

So, what does it mean?

You reach for your dictionary. Enough – sufficient, adequate. That doesn't sound very good. I am sufficient. I am adequate. You reach in deeper, but what does that mean? Adequate – mediocre. I am mediocre?

Now, do you feel inspired and motivated, or do you feel small and insignificant?

Whenever I hear someone say, "You are enough", I can't help myself. I yell out, "I'm not."

Why do we say these things? Why do we tell children that they are not perfect? Why do we limit them to being enough? Why do we limit ourselves?

In fact, I am infinitely magnificent.

Rather than enough, I choose to be magnificent. If we look at the word "magnificent", it means "great, elevated, noble, distinguished," literally "doing great deeds" and "living in splendour."

Yes! That is something I can aspire to be.

Three years ago, not long before I read this sign, my grandson Mason was born. When I held him in my arms for the first time, I looked at his sweet little perfect face. He is so perfect with such infinite potential within him.

In that split second, I could see him from this tiny baby, not even an hour old, as a toddler, a child, a teenager, and a young man. He wrapped his arms around me, and I heard his voice, "Thank you, Grandma, for teaching me to believe in myself."

I question how my beautiful, perfect Mason could become imperfect by age 12. Of course, his behaviour may not always be perfect, and he sometimes drives us a little crazy. However, if he is perfect as a newborn, isn't he always going to be perfect? How could he go from having this infinite potential as this perfect newborn to just enough?

This infinite possibility is not just his to explore and maybe get to in the future. It is him now. It is who he is – the innovator, the explainer, the verifier, the achiever and the genius. He is that now and will be that when he is old. It will always be him, so how can he ever be just enough? He is now and will always be infinitely magnificent.

We don't know what the full potential of being human is. We have no idea. My research led me around in circles. No one knows.

Let's look at some of the infinitely magnificent achievements by humans,

The four-minute mile was thought to be impossible to break until Roger Bannister ran 3.59.4 minutes in 1954, and now it is 3:43 minutes.

Automobiles were new in 1903, but the Wright brothers didn't say this was enough. They took to the skies.

Going to the moon was impossible when JFK deemed they would reach it. And man has walked on the moon. Now the race is on to send a team of women to Mars.

Do you think any people involved in these achievements thought they were enough? They knew their potential would only be limited by thinking they were enough. They knew their potential was way beyond what they could see and kept on going.

Whenever someone says that something is impossible, someone else will go out and prove them wrong. Someone will always recognise they are more than they ever need to be. They know they have infinite magnificence and will take that extra step, going the extra mile to make the impossible possible.

Always remember you are more than you will ever need to be. You will never just enough. You are infinitely magnificent.

As a Social Mission Revolutionist, you must look outside what you think is possible. Look beyond what you have been capable of in the past. This is no longer your ceiling. When you get started, it may be small. It will pull you and test you in unimaginable ways.

You have not chosen this path. This path has chosen you. Your social mission has been waiting for you. This means that everything that you need to be, you are. You will climb the highest mountains and navigate the roughest seas. However, it is your path, and you will do it perfectly.

When I talk about being perfect, that doesn't mean we don't make mistakes. I make plenty. It means that you are perfectly designed for what lies ahead. You are who you are meant to be. Even your mistakes will perfectly guide you into the next breakthrough.

Never doubt your perfection. Always hold on to your infinite magnificence and allow it to lead the way beyond your wildest dreams.

You were never enough!

You are INFINITELY MAGNIFICENT.

A Social Mission Revolutionist
is waiting to be born
within each of us.

CHAPTER 9

Follow Your Heart

As I was completing this book, I asked my mother, "Is it important for people to make a difference?"

Mum is now 85 and becoming frail. She has lived a life of service, caring and offering compassion to everyone she interacts with. While her mobility is limited, I see her taking time to touch people's lives in any way she can.

Her response to me was, "as long as they don't expect to do it by big strokes, just small steps. I think that's what we need to do."

She continued to tell me about how she makes an effort to stop and talk with people. When she goes to the shop and sees someone in the street who she feels could use a kind word, she will stop and chat with them.

I asked her the question I ask everyone, "If there was one thing you could fight for, what would it be? Her immediate response was, "I'm not a fighter."

She continued, "You've got to be kind to people. If it's just talking to a stranger in the street, there's no harm in that. That's being responsive to their need at the time to have someone to talk to. People have to be willing to change their attitude and learn. When they do, they become more caring and can connect with others better."

This is who my mother is. Whenever she is in hospital, as soon as she can get up, with the help of a walker if she needs to, she'll be off on her social mission of talking with people, helping them to feel less lonely in their isolation from home. She gives them an ear to listen to and shows them that someone cares.

Her advice for the world is simple. Be Kind.

There is a purpose in sharing this conversation with my mum. I wanted to highlight to you that no matter who you are and what circumstances in life you find yourself in, there is something that you can do that will make a difference in another's life.

This is what gives you a sense of purpose in life. It is how my mother keeps going when her health is failing and life feels challenging. She thinks of others and tends to their needs within her capacity.

What is it that you can do right now to have a positive impact on someone's life? You just may change their world.

A Social Mission Revolutionist is waiting to be born within each of us.

The world is crying out for love and compassion. Taking time to find our **Compassionate Purpose** is one of the most important things we can do. If each of us does one thing, following that passion that pulls and tugs at us, we will have a world filled with compassion where all are cared for. Can you imagine it?

We are all on a journey of discovery. Step by step, our lives unfold to reveal the gold that will allow us to shine brightly. We shine the brightest when we put aside our wants and desires and start to focus on what we have been gifted with that we can share with the world.

For each of us, it is something different. We have unique gifts, skills and talents that make up who we are. Our calling in life takes in every aspect of these. Whatever your experience in life, whether perceived as good or bad, gives you a perspective you can share with others.

Opening up to the idea of finding your social mission gives you insight into yourself. While not intended to be about personal growth and development, it is the ultimate teacher in this area. You will grow and stretch yourself beyond your imagination. You will find a tremendous sense of fulfilment and joy in the art of giving of yourself.

The social mission that each of us is called to is unique and powerful. You might have thought, "There isn't much I can do".

Hopefully, in reading this book, your eyes will have been opened to discover that no matter how small an action appears, it can and will make a difference.

The stories I have shared have been diverse in many ways. Some have been small actions. Others have become bigger than their founders dare to dream. However, they have all started with that one small step. Very few have any idea of what they are doing or where it is going to take them when they start. The call is so great when they hear or feel it. It sets them on fire with the compulsion that *I can't not do this*.

Listen to the stories on the podcast episodes I have shared. These are just a selection. Many others will inspire you and possibly open your eyes to other ways you can get involved.

Throughout the book, you have been guided to discover what your social mission may be. Has it sparked something within? Is there a sense of uneasiness that there is something you must do? Even if you are not sure yet what it is, you have had an awakening that will bring you the greatest sense of fulfilment and joy in your life.

It will disrupt you. It will change the way you think about yourself and the way you act. It is a disruption that, in time, you will be grateful for.

You may feel that starting your social mission is too much. That's OK. You don't have to. When you listen to the podcasts, you may be inspired to get involved and support someone else's social mission.

This may be your **Compassionate Purpose**. We all need help in some way or another and would appreciate your assistance. Working through the process outlined in this book gives you a better idea of where you belong and what your heart is calling you to do.

In whatever way you are called, it is perfect. You just need to follow.

Listen closely to that inner calling. It is there waiting for you. It will show you the way to an immense sense of fulfilment and joy you have ever known. All you need to do is follow your heart.

Bibliography

Moll, Dr J. Krueger, F. Zahn, R. Pardini, M. de Oliveira-Souza, R & Grafman, J. 2006, *Human fronto–mesolimbic networks guide decisions about charitable donation*. National Academy of Sciences, Washington, USA.

Post, Dr S. 2011, *It's good to be good: 2011 5th annual scientific report on health, happiness and helping others,* The International Journal of Person-Centered Medicine.

Post, Dr S. & Niemark, J. 2007, *Why Good Things Happen to Good People*, Broadway Books, New York City.

The 2021-2022 National Study of Mental Health and Wellbeing (NSMHW) is a component of the wider Intergenerational Health and Mental Health Study (IHMHS) funded by the Australian Government Department of Health and conducted by the Australian Bureau of Statistics.

Gallup 2021, *State of the Global Workplace Engagement Report 2021, Gallup Headquarters, Washington, USA*

Cole, S & Fredrickson, B. Hill. *Stanford Medical School's Center for Compassion and Altruism Research and Education's (CCARE) inaugural Science of Compassion conference*, 2012.

Index

Acts of Service, 71
Alex Dekker, 62
Arthur Aron, 42
Beyond the Why, 91
Bianca Cefalo, 56
Cascie Kambouris, 73
Chocolate and Coffee Breaks, 43
Chocolate and Coffee Day for Religious Harmony, 42
Dr Arun Dhir, 35
Dr Jorge Moll, 27
Dr Stephen Post,, 29
Frank McKinney, 21
Giving Gifts, 73
Giving Heals, 35
Health and Mental Health, 30
IWillRideWithYou, 40
Karen Palmer, 51
Kevin Milstein, 49
Languages of Social Mission, 67
legacy, 24
Lillian Brummet, 65
Lindt Chocolate Café, 38
Passions, 87
Peter Nicholls, 59
Physical Touch, 75
Quality Time, 74
Randa Haverliah, 50
Robert Akeroyd, 53
Sarfia Altono Younes and Hassan Younes, 48
Scott Carson, 61
Sean Bell, 55
Shannon Hurley, 54
Shelly Galvin, 95
Stories, 81
Strengths, 83
Tina Murray, 47
Ubuntu, 16
Ultimate Impact, 89
Values, 88
Vera Entwistle, 63

About the Author

Andrea Putting is an international speaker, author and trusted advisor to Authentic Influencers. Through her keynote speeches, books, programs and podcasts, she guides individuals and businesses in building co-creative communities and adopting social missions.

After studying Naturopathy and Homoeopathy, Andrea started her business as an early adopter of the online world. When she sold this business, she entered the workforce as an employee. Here she discovered a world that also needed healing. Her deep exploration led her to the Social Mission Revolution.

Since 2019, Andrea has been championing the causes of passionate people making a difference in the world through her podcast, *Social Mission Revolution*. The podcast highlights inspirational people and businesses who have an **Authentic influence** on the world through social mission.

When we combine our passions, something magical can be created. Andrea's passions and values came together to create her social mission, where people can come together to break down barriers. Chocolate and Coffee Day for Religious Harmony began on 15 December 2015. Chocolate and Coffee Breaks evolved in 2020 to transform situations where there are feelings of nonacceptance and misunderstanding into building a community spirit.

Andrea was awarded the Toastmaster of the Year in her local club in 2016. She was honoured with awards as the Best Volunteer and Best Tribe Member in global awards with Speakers Tribe in 2020 and nominated as Best Leader in 2021. She received a Wordsmith award at the Innov8 Awards in 2021.

Andrea's writings have inspired and challenged people over the internet for over 20 years. As an author, she has written *"Awakened Stealth Leadership – A Soulful Approach to Growing People and Organisations,"* inspired by more than four decades of experience in leadership, the award-winning and best-selling *"Compassionate Prosperity, When*

Success is Not Enough" and *"Moment of Infinity, Anthology of Daily Devotionals."* She has also provided chapters in various books and written many published articles.

Andrea Putting lives in Melbourne, Australia, amongst the gumtrees, kangaroos and cockatoos with her husband and pet cockatoo, Fella. She has two adult children and two grandchildren who keep her jumping in puddles.

For further information on
Compassionate Purpose
visit www.AndreaPutting.com

Chocolate and Coffee Breaks

Chocolate, coffee and conversation – what a delicious combination! It incites deep sensuous emotions and experiences, which take us out of the daily grind and lift us into a place of belonging and acceptance. It is a simple way to make a difference and become an **Authentic Influence**.

If you can make one person smile and lift their spirits when they feel lonely, isolated, or depressed, something shifts in the whole universe.

Reaching one person is simple. Chocolate and Coffee Day for Religious Harmony and Chocolate and Coffee Breaks create connections that allow this to happen.

Sharing chocolate and a cuppa with someone is part of our daily life. It transcends all cultures. There is something about sitting with someone else with a cup in our hands. In doing this, we meet each other as equals.

The warmth of the liquid allows us to open up and speak more freely and compassionately than we might otherwise do. It brings us into a place of listening, ready to hear the other's story. It allows us to be prepared to open up to find the similarities that help us connect.

When we share these simple pleasures of life, something magical happens. We can break down barriers that divide us.

Sharing in **Chocolate and Coffee Breaks** opens us up to creating communities where we all feel accepted, have a sense of belonging, and are provided with an opportunity to contribute. These are essential parts of our being. Wherever there are any nonacceptance and misunderstanding feelings, it is time for a **Chocolate and Coffee Break**.

Chocolate and Coffee Day for Religious Harmony is held annually on 15 December. However, any day of the year is a good day for a **Chocolate and Coffee Break**.

Visit www.ChocolateandCoffeeBreaks.com for ideas and conversation starters and explore how you, your community or your business can get involved. You can also invite Andrea Putting to facilitate a Chocolate and Coffee Event for you.

Social Mission Revolution Podcast

Social Mission Revolution Podcast began in 2019. Since then, Andrea has interviewed people from all walks of life involved in social missions. Their stories are varied and cover a wide diversity of worthy causes.

Listen to the podcast at
www.SocialMissionRevolution.com
or watch on YouTube.

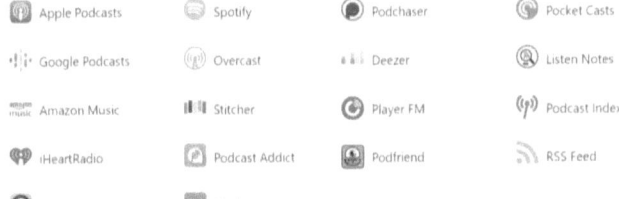

www.ingramcontent.com/pod-product-compliance
Lightning Source LLC
Chambersburg PA
CBHW030259010526
44107CB00053B/1764